Gratefully presented to

<u>Pastor Gary Bazr</u>

by

<u>Those who love him</u> ♡

on

<u>This day which the Lord hath given us</u> ☺

Hope you enjoy this and are encouraged and challenged by these thoughts!

All Preachers GREAT & Small

A Pastor's Appreciation Book

Compiled by Gary Wilde

Harold Shaw Publishers
Wheaton, Illinois

© 1996 by Harold Shaw Publishers

All Scripture quotations, unless otherwise indicated, are taken from *The Holy Bible: New International Version.* Copyright © 1973, 1978, 1984 by the International Bible Society. Used by permission of Zondervan Publishing House.

Scripture quotations marked NRSV are from the *New Revised Standard Version of the Bible,* copyrighted 1989 by the Division of Christian Education of the National Council of the Churches of Christ in the United States of America, and are used by permission. All rights reserved.

ISBN 0-87788-143-X

Compiled by Gary Wilde

Cover design by David LaPlaca

Library of Congress Cataloging-in-Publication Data

All preachers great and small / compiled by Gary Wilde.
    p. cm.
  ISBN 0-87788-143-X
  1. Clergy—Office—Quotations, maxims, etc. 2. Preaching—Quotations, maxims, etc. I. Wilde, Gary.
BV660.2.A35 1996
253—dc20   96-8400
                                                      CIP

---

03 02 01 00 99 98 97 96

10 9 8 7 6 5 4 3 2 1

CONTENTS

Life in the World

Devotional Life

Pastoral Life

Personal Life

LIFE IN THE WORLD

Cultivating Awareness and Wonder

The world will never starve for want of wonders, but for want of wonder.

G. K. Chesterton

A greater poverty than that caused by lack of money is the poverty of awareness. Men and women go about the world unaware of the beauty, the goodness, in it. Their souls are poor. It is better to have a poor pocketbook than to suffer from a poor soul.

Thomas Dreier

He who can no longer pause to wonder and stand rapt in awe is as good as dead; his eyes are closed.

Albert Einstein

What do they know of heaven or hell, Cathy, who know nothing of life?

Laurence Olivier, in the movie Wuthering Heights

O LORD, our Lord, how majestic is your name in all the earth!
You have set your glory above the heavens.
From the lips of children and infants you have ordained praise
because of your enemies, to silence the foe and the avenger.
When I consider your heavens, the work of your fingers,
the moon and the stars, which you have set in place,
what is man that you are mindful of him,
the son of man that you care for him?
You made him a little lower than the heavenly beings
and crowned him with glory and honor.
You made him ruler over the works of your hands;
you put everything under his feet:
all flocks and herds, and the beasts of the field,
the birds of the air, and the fish of the sea,
all that swim the paths of the seas.
O LORD, our Lord, how majestic is your name in all the earth!

Psalm 8

There are glimpses of heaven to us in every act, or thought, or word,
that raises us above ourselves.

Arthur P. Stanley

Every experience in life, everything with which we have come in contact in life, is a chisel which has been cutting away at our life statue, molding, modifying, shaping it. We are part of all we have met.

Orison Swett Marden

I find that most professionals, and especially most men, hold a mild skepticism toward the faith. They feel that something abstract like faith can't stand the rigors of the street. They attend church on Sunday, and so forth. But religion is a sort of weekend hobby, like golf or fishing. Come Monday, it's time to put away those toys and get back to the "real world."

Doug Sherman and William Hendricks, Your Work Matters to God

"You must learn to look at the world twice," Indian elders advise. First you must bring your eyes together in front so you can see each droplet of rain on the grass, so you can see the smoke rising from an ant hill in the sunshine. *Nothing* should escape your notice. But you must learn to look again, with your eyes at the very edge of what is visible. Now you must see dimly if you wish to see things that are dim—visions, mist, and cloud people, animals which hurry past you

in the dark. You must learn to look at the world twice if you wish to
see all that there is to see.

Jamake Highwater, in Warrior Wisdom

While with an eye made quiet by the power
Of harmony, and the deep power of joy,
We see into the life of things.

William Wordsworth

It seems to me we can never give up longing and wishing while we
are thoroughly alive. There are certain things we feel to be beautiful
and good, and we must hunger after them.

George Eliot

Each one sees what he carries in his heart.

Johann Wolfgang von Goethe

Every one of us has had experiences which we have not been able to
explain: a sudden sense of loneliness, or a feeling of wonder or awe in
the face of the universal vastness. Or we have had a fleeting visitation

of light like an illumination from some other sun, giving us in a quick flash an assurance that we are from another world, that our origins are divine. . . . We were forced to suspend our acquired doubts while, for a moment, the clouds were rolled back and we saw and heard for ourselves.

A. W. Tozer, The Pursuit of God

The heavens declare the glory of God;
the skies proclaim the work of his hands.
Day after day they pour forth speech;
night after night they display knowledge.
There is no speech or language where their voice is not heard.
Their voice goes out into all the earth,
their words to the ends of the world.
In the heavens he has pitched a tent for the sun,
which is like a bridegroom coming forth from his pavilion,
like a champion rejoicing to run his course.
It rises at one end of the heavens and makes its circuit to the other;
nothing is hidden from its heat.

Psalm 19:1-6

Preaching in Today's World

"Don't preach to me!" means "Don't bore me to death with your offensive platitudes." Respectable verbs don't get into that kind of trouble entirely by accident. Sermons are like jokes; even the best ones are hard to remember. In both cases that may be just as well. Ideally the thing to remember is not the preachers' eloquence but the lump in your throat or the heart in your mouth or the thorn in your flesh that appeared as much in spite of what they said as because of it.

Frederick Buechner, Wishful Thinking

Today we have sermonettes, by preacherettes, for Christianettes.

Charles F. Taylor

I well remember Jock Purves saying that he felt one of the greatest things John Knox ever did was to dismiss an audience with just the benediction. He preached no sermon at all because he had no word from the Lord for the people. Most of us would have warmed up an old sermon.

Leonard Ravenhill, Revival Praying

There are few wild beasts more to be dreaded than a communicative man having nothing to communicate.

Christian Nestell Bovee

One of the proofs of the divinity of our gospel is the preaching it has survived.

Woodrow Wilson

Pastoral conversation is not merely a skillful use of conversational techniques to manipulate people in the Kingdom of God, but a deep human encounter in which a man is willing to put his own hope and despair, his own light and darkness at the disposal of others who want to find a way through their confusion and touch the solid core of life. In this context preaching means more than handing over a tradition; it is rather the careful and sensitive articulation of what is happening in the community so that those who listen can say: "You say what I suspected, you express what I vaguely felt, you bring to the fore what I fearfully kept in the back of my mind. Yes, yes, you say who we are, you recognize our condition.

Henri Nouwen, The Wounded Healer

The prophet is a man who feels fiercely. God has thrust a burden upon his soul, and he is bowed and stunned at man's fierce greed. Frightful is the agony of man; no human voice can convey its full terror. Prophecy is the voice that God has lent to the silent agony, a voice to the plundered poor, to the profaned riches of the world. It is a form of living, a crossing point of God and man. God is raging in the prophets words.

Abraham Joshua Heschel, in Warrior Wisdom

If you would be pungent, be brief; for it is with words as with sunbeams—the more they are condensed, the deeper they burn.

Robert Southey

Noise proves nothing. Often a hen who has merely laid an egg cackles as if she had laid an asteroid.

Mark Twain

There's a great power in words, if you don't hitch too many of them together.

Josh Billings

True eloquence does not consist in speech. Words and phrases may be marshalled in every way, but they cannot compass it. It must consist in the man, in the subject, and in the occasion. It comes, if at all, like the outbreaking of a fountain from the earth, or the bursting forth of volcanic fires, with spontaneous, original native force.

Daniel Webster

That must be wonderful; I have no idea of what it means.

Jean Baptiste Poquelin Molière

The test of a preacher is that his congregation goes away saying not "What a lovely sermon" but, "I will do something!"

Francis de Sales

Confronting Prejudice and Racism

I refuse to accept the idea that the "isness" of man's present nature makes him morally incapable of reaching up for the "oughtness" that forever confronts him.

Martin Luther King, Jr.

The fact that homogeneous churches grow faster does not necessarily mean they are best. It's tempting to justify our weaknesses rather than reach out effectively. What kind of witness is a large, homogeneous church whose gospel is not strong enough to lead people to work to overcome a human weakness as obvious as racial prejudice?

John Perkins, in Leadership Handbooks of Practical Theology

Beware prejudices. They are like rats, and men's minds are like traps; prejudices get in easily, but it is doubtful if they ever get out.

Lord Jeffrey

It appears that the strategy of Christ was to win the loyalty of the few who would honestly respond to the new way of living. They would be the pioneers of the new order, the spearhead of advance against the massed ignorance, selfishness, evil, "play acting" and apathy of the majority of the human race. The goal which was set before them, for which they were to work and pray and—if need be—suffer and die, was the building of a new Kingdom of inner supreme loyalty, the Kingdom of God. This was to transcend every barrier of race—and frontier of time and space as well.

J. B. Phillips, Your God Is Too Small

In Christ Jesus you are all children of God through faith. As many of you as were baptized into Christ have clothed yourselves with Christ. There is no longer Jew or Greek, there is no longer slave or free, there is no longer male and female; for all of you are one in Christ Jesus. And if you belong to Christ, then you are Abraham's offspring, heirs according to the promise.

Galatians 3:26-29, NRSV

Sadly, many of our children are infected with a highly developed racial value system at an early age. An African couple from our church enrolled their five-year-old in a daycare center at a white church. When the leader of a local soup kitchen was shot and killed (an incident that devastated our entire city), the daycare's head teacher, who was white, talked to the children about what had happened. For some reason, she emphasized that the murderer was black. At home that night, our church members' daughter asked her parents, "Why are black people bad?"

Spencer Perkins, More than Equals

It is the duty of the younger Negro artist . . . to change through the force of his art that old whispering "I want to be white," hidden in the aspiration of his people, to "Why should I want to be white? I am a Negro—and beautiful!"

Langston Hughes

I have a dream that one day this nation will rise up and live out the true meaning of its creed: "We hold these truths to be self-evident that all men are created equal." I have a dream that my four little children will one day live in a nation where they will not be judged by the color of their skin but by the content of their character. I have a dream today.

Martin Luther King, Jr.

When dealing with people, remember you are not dealing with creatures of logic, but with creatures of emotion, creatures bristling with prejudice, and motivated by pride and vanity.

Dale Carnegie

Sex prejudice is so ingrained in our society that many who practice it are simply unaware that they are hurting women. It is the last socially acceptable prejudice.

Bernice Sandler

Though the church in the past has repudiated its Florence Nightingales and treated its Dorothy Sayerses as not quite human, we sincerely hope that in the future it will give its daughters their full inheritance as the children of God. We can no longer simply smile condescendingly at the oft-quoted prayer of the little girl, "Dear God, are boys better than girls? I know you are one, but try to be fair." Rather, we must assure Sylvia, who offered this prayer, that God is just as much like her as like a boy and that some day she may not only speak *to* God in prayer as a Christian, but also *for* him as a minister of the gospel, proclaiming to all who hear her that God is, indeed, a God who is fair.

Paul K. Jewett, The Ordination of Women

"Blessed be God," says the Jew, "that hath not made me a woman." God, of course, may have his own opinion, but the church is reluctant to endorse it. I think I have never heard a sermon preached on the story of Martha and Mary that did not attempt, somehow, somewhere, to explain away its text. Mary's, of course, was the better part—the Lord said so, and we must not precisely contradict him. But we will be careful not to despise Martha. No doubt, he approved of her, too. We could not get on without her, and indeed (having paid lip-service to God's opinion) we must admit that we greatly prefer her. For Martha was doing a really feminine job, whereas Mary was just behaving like any other disciple, male or female; and that is a hard pill to swallow. Perhaps it is no wonder that the women were first at the Cradle and last at the Cross.

Dorothy Sayers, Are Women Human?

A little girl asked her Sunday school teacher: "Why do they always say 'amen' after they pray in church? Why don't they ever say 'a-woman'?" Before the teacher could think of an answer, a little boy in the class spoke up and said: "They do that for the same reason that all the songs they sing are 'hims.'"

Anonymous

Christianity doesn't require any power when its only challenge is to do something that already comes naturally. But it will take a powerful gospel—a gospel with guts—to enable us to love across all the barriers we erect to edify our own kind and protect us from our insecurities.

Spencer Perkins, More than Equals

The Pilgrim mother endured all the trials the Pilgrim fathers endured, but in addition, endured the Pilgrim fathers.

Anonymous

Christians understand that if anyone has the mandate to do something about the problem of race, it is the followers of Christ. A major part of our witness to the unbelieving world lies in our ability to demonstrate a message powerful enough to cut through our racial baggage and present to the world a body where Jew and Gentile, male and female, slave and free, can all drink from the same cup.

John Perkins, in Leadership Handbooks of Practical Theology

For he himself is our peace, who has made the two one and has destroyed the barrier, the dividing wall of hostility, by abolishing in his flesh the law with its commandments and regulations. His purpose was to create in himself one new man out of the two, thus making peace, and in this one body to reconcile both of them to God through the cross, by which he put to death their hostility. He came and preached peace to you who were far away and peace to those who were near.

Ephesians 2:14-17

I have fought against white domination, and I have fought against black domination. I have cherished the ideal of a democratic and free society in which all persons will live together in harmony and with equal opportunities. It is an ideal which I hope to live for and achieve. But, if needs be, it is an ideal for which I am prepared to die.

Nelson Mandela, at his trial on April 20, 1964

A great many people think they are thinking when they are merely rearranging their prejudices.

William James

You're either part of the solution or part of the problem.

Eldridge Cleaver

Dealing with the Tough Times

God whispers to us in our pleasures, speaks in our conscience, but shouts in our pains: it is His megaphone to rouse a deaf world.

C. S. Lewis, The Problem of Pain

No words can express how much the world owes to sorrow. Most of the psalms were born in a wilderness. Most of the epistles were written in a prison. The greatest thoughts of the greatest thinkers have all passed through the fire. . . . Take comfort, afflicted Christian! When God is about to make preeminent use of a man, He puts him in the fire.

George MacDonald

Because I have to walk with a stick and have only one hand free, I'm more nuisance than help and can only sit on the sidelines and give advice and be a pest. It *is* difficult having to accept all the time! But unless we did, how could others have the pleasure, and the spiritual growth, of giving? And—I don't know about you, but I was very proud; I liked the superior feeling of helping others, and for me it is much harder to receive that to give but, I think, much more blessed.

Joy Davidman, dying of cancer, in And God Came In

Where there is sorrow, there is holy ground.

Oscar Wilde

Do not worry about anything, but in everything by prayer and supplication with thanksgiving let your requests be made known to God. And the peace of God, which surpasses all understanding, will guard your hearts and your minds in Christ Jesus.

Philippians 4:6-7, NRSV

In a presumably perfect world, there would be no depression, no suffering, no pain, not even any death. But this brave new world would be lifeless. It would be static and pointless, full of a hypnotically dull and relentless sameness. If we all had perfect bodies and perfect minds, the joy of individual difference and mutual discovery would disappear. We would know exactly what to expect, as we do of machines, for only machines can be perfect.

Leslie Hazleton, The Right to Feel Bad

I have a new philosophy. I'm only going to dread one day at a time.

Charlie Brown

One afternoon while playing on a wooden picnic table, four-year-old Jordon ran a splinter into his finger. Sobbing, he called his father (me) at the office. "I want God to take the splinter out," he said. I told him his mother could remove it very easily. But he wanted God to do it because when Mom takes a splinter out, it hurts. He wanted God to remove it "by himself." When I got home an hour later, the splinter was still there, so I proceeded to remove it, and I tried to teach Jordon that sometimes God uses others to do his work. And sometimes it is painful.

Illustrations for Teaching and Preaching

Dear friends, do not be surprised at the painful trial you are suffering, as though something strange were happening to you. But rejoice that you participate in the sufferings of Christ, so that you may be overjoyed when his glory is revealed. If you are insulted because of the name of Christ, you are blessed, for the Spirit of glory and of God rests on you. If you suffer, it should not be as a murderer or thief or any other kind of criminal, or even as a meddler. However, if you suffer as a Christian, do not be ashamed, but praise God that you bear that name. For it is time for judgment to begin with the family of God; and if it begins with us, what will the outcome be for those who do not obey the gospel of God?

1 Peter 4:12-17

I prefer a description like "victorious battle" to "victorious life" because the latter is apt to leave the false impression that Christians have no problems. There are struggles. . . . You know that cold-mashed-potatoes feeling that comes when you wake up and begin to remember all your problems?

Paul Little, How to Give Away Your Faith

We are all faced with great opportunities . . . brilliantly disguised as impossible situations.

Truett Cathy, founder of Chick-Fil-A restaurants

Not only creativeness and enjoyment are meaningful. If there is a meaning in life at all, then there must be a meaning in suffering. Suffering is an ineradicable part of life, even as fate and death. Without suffering and death, human life cannot be complete.

Victor Frankl

I needed that scratch to awaken me.

Tyrone Power, during a fencing match in the movie The Mark of Zorro

We do not need the sheltering wings when things go smoothly. We are closest to God in the darkness, stumbling along blindly.

Madeleine L'Engle

As an example of suffering and patience, beloved, take the prophets who spoke in the name of the Lord. Indeed, we call blessed those who showed endurance. You have heard of the endurance of Job, and you have seen the purpose of the Lord, how the Lord is compassionate and merciful.

James 5:10-11, NRSV

Only eyes washed by tears can see clearly.

Louis L. Mann

Is there any greater wretchedness than to taste the dregs of our own insufficiency and misery and hopelessness, and to know that we are certainly worth nothing at all? Yet it is blessed to be reduced to these depths if, in them, we can find God. Until we have reached the bottom of the abyss, there is still something for us to choose between all and nothing. There is still something in-between. We can still evade the decision. When we are reduced to our last extreme, there is no further evasion. The choice is a terrible one. It is made in the heart of darkness, but with an intuition that is unbearable by its angelic clarity: when we who have been destroyed and seem to be in hell miraculously choose God!

Thomas Merton, No Man Is an Island

There was peace in their hearts. They were filled with the fearlessness of those who have lost *everything,* the fearlessness which is not easy to come by but which endures.

Alexander Solzhenitsyn, The First Circle

Extending Compassion

God dwells among the lowliest people. He sits on the dust heap among the prison convicts. With the juvenile delinquents He stands at the door, begging bread. He throngs with the beggars at the place of alms. He is among the sick. He stands in line with the unemployed. Therefore, let him who would meet God visit the prison cell before going to the Temple. Before he goes to church let him visit the hospital. Before he reads his Bible let him help the beggar standing at his door.

Kagawa

Compassion is the sometimes fatal capacity for feeling what it's like to live inside somebody else's skin. It is the knowledge that there can never really be any peace and joy for me until there is peace and joy finally for you too.

Frederick Buechner, Wishful Thinking

We awaken in others the same attitude of mind we hold toward them.
Elbert Hubbard

The value of compassion cannot be over-emphasized. Anyone can criticize. It takes a true believer to be compassionate. No greater burden can be borne by an individual than to know no one cares or understands.

Arthur H. Stainback

Then the righteous will answer him, "Lord, when did we see you hungry and feed you, or thirsty and give you something to drink? When did we see you a stranger and invite you in, or needing clothes and clothe you? When did we see you sick or in prison and go to visit you?" The King will reply, "I tell you the truth, whatever you did for one of the least of these brothers of mine, you did for me."

Matthew 25:37-40

What does love look like? It has the hands to help others. It has the feet to hasten to the poor and needy. It has the eyes to see misery and want. It has the ears to hear sighs and sorrows. That is what love looks like.

Augustine

A young Amish girl received a small box of candy for Christmas. Her mother, teaching her unselfishness, suggested she keep the candy unopened until her friends came by. After several weeks, her friends came, and she excitedly passed the candy around, with each taking a piece. She closed the box and set it on the table without taking a piece herself. When her mother asked her if she wanted some of the candy, she blushed and said, "Oh, I forgot that I was here."

Anonymous

Faith without ethical consequences is a lie. Good works must necessarily follow faith. God does not need our sacrifices, but he has, nevertheless, appointed a representative to receive them, namely our neighbor. The neighbor always represents the invisible Christ.

J. S. Whale, Christian Doctrine

DEVOTIONAL LIFE

Sustaining Fellowship with the Lord

The man who has no inner life is the slave of his surroundings.

Henri Frederic Amiel

The hardest thing about clerical sanctity is that you don't have to have it—and you can get along beautifully. *Only you and God will know.* You can fake the spiritual life.

Father John-Julian, speaking to candidates for ministry

All human beings pass away. Do not let your happiness depend on something you may lose. If love is to be a blessing, not a misery, it must be for the only beloved who will never pass away.

C. S. Lewis, The Four Loves

The secret and reality of this blissful life in God cannot be understood without receiving, living, and experiencing it. If we try to understand it only with the intellect, we will find our effort useless. A scientist had a bird in his hand. He saw that it had life, and, wanting to find out in what part of the bird's body the life was, he began dissecting the bird. The result was that the very life of which he was in search disappeared mysteriously. Those who try to understand the inner life merely intellectually will meet with a similar failure. The life for which they are looking will vanish in the analysis.

Sundar Singh, in Richard Foster's Devotional Classics

We can view spirituality as friendship with God. As we do so, these two themes—God is holy and God is personal—must both be held in our minds, existing in a dynamic tension. If not, there is the danger that we will remake God into a celestial buddy who pals around with us, or we will be so intimidated by His awesome power that we will never draw close.

James Osterhaus, Bonds of Iron

The soul needs an intense, full-bodied spiritual life as much as and in the same way that the body needs food. That is the teaching and imagery of spiritual matters over centuries. But these same masters demonstrate that the spiritual life requires careful attention, because it can be dangerous. It's easy to go crazy in the life of the spirit, warring against those who disagree, proselytizing for our own personal attachments rather than expressing our own soulfulness, or taking narcissistic satisfactions in our belief rather than finding meaning and pleasure in spirituality that is available to everyone.

Thomas Moore, Care of the Soul

In our TV ads, it is as though the ecstasy of the spirit experienced by a St. Theresa or a St. Francis can be reduced to the gratification coming from a particular car, and the kind of love that Christ compared to His love for His church can be expressed by buying the right kind of wrist watch "for that special person in your life." . . . Hitherto, spiritual gratification could come only via spiritual means. Thus, people were urged to choose between the things of this world and the blessings of God. Now, that duality has been overcome. Ours is an age in which spiritual blessings are being promised to those who buy material things. The spiritual is being absorbed by the physical. The fruit of the Spirit, suggests the media, can be had without God and without spiritual disciplines.

Tony Campolo, Wake Up America

Seeing God as parent may seem childish. But might there be, in the unadmitted sparkle of the child within you, a sometime longing to climb into God's fatherly lap, to nestle against God's motherly breast, to rest for a moment in the shadow of God's wings or be held in God's strong and tender arms? If you could allow yourself to feel it, are there not times when you would love to cry on God's shoulder, to let God tell you you are worthwhile and beautiful? And is there not something in you that would be delighted if you could bring a smile to God's face?

Gerald May, The Awakened Heart

For I tell you this: One loving blind desire for God alone is more valuable in itself, more pleasing to God and to the saints, more beneficial to your own growth, and more helpful to your friends, both living and dead, than anything else you could do.

The Cloud of Unknowing

Making Time for Reading and Study

Reading is a basic tool in the living of a good life.

Mortimer J. Adler

The soul, like the body, lives by what it feeds on.

Josiah Gilbert Holland

The noblest exercise of the mind within doors, and most befitting a person of quality, is study.

William Ramsay

The mind of the scholar, if he would leave it large and liberal, should come in contact with other minds.

Henry Wadsworth Longfellow

On earth, man wears himself out in intellectual adventures, as though seeking to take wing and fly to infinity. Motionless before his desk, he

edges his way closer, ever closer, to the borders of the spirit, in constant mortal danger of plunging into the void. At such times—though
very rarely—the spirit, too, has its glimpses of the dawn light.

Yokio Mioshima

The more we study the more we discover our ignorance.

Percy Bysshe Shelley

No student knows his subject; the most he knows is where and how
to find out the things he does not know.

Woodrow Wilson

Our delight in any particular study, art, or science rises and improves
in proportion to the application which we bestow upon it. Thus, what
was at first an exercise becomes at length an entertainment.

Joseph Addison

Nurture your mind with great thoughts. To believe in the heroic
makes heroes.

Benjamin Disraeli

To say nothing of its holiness or authority, the Bible contains more specimens of genius and taste than any other volume in existence.

Walter S. Landor

Your word is a lamp to my feet and a light to my path. I have sworn an oath and confirmed it, to observe your righteous ordinances.

Psalm 119:105-106, NRSV

The Bible is a window in this prison of hope, through which we look into eternity.

John Sullivan Dwight

We should be as careful of the books we read as of the company we keep. The dead very often have more power than the living.

Tryon Edwards

Some people never learn anything because they understand everything too soon.

Alexander Pope

I hate television. I hate it as much as peanuts. But I can't stop eating peanuts.

Orson Welles

I could give no reply except a lazy and drowsy, "Yes, Lord, yes, I'll get to it right away; just don't bother me for a little while." But "right away" didn't happen right away; and a "little while" turned out to be a very long while.

Augustine of Hippo

Reason should be viewed not as a source of knowledge and contrasted with revelation, but as a means of comprehending revelation.

Carl F. H. Henry

Persevering in Prayer

We all pray whether we think of it as praying or not. The odd silence
we fall into when something very beautiful is happening. . . . The
stammer of pain at somebody else's pain. The stammer of joy at somebody else's joy. Whatever words or sounds we use for sighing with
over our own lives. These are all prayers in their way.

Frederick Buechner, Wishful Thinking

The progress to consummation of God's work in this world has two
basic principles: God's ability to give and man's ability to ask. Failure
in either one is fatal to the success of God's work on earth. God's
inability to do or to give would put an end to redemption. Man's failure to pray would, just as surely, set a limit to the plan. But God's ability to do and to give has never failed and cannot fail; but man's
ability to ask can fail, and often does. Therefore the slow progress
which is being made toward the realization of a world won for Christ
lies entirely with man's limited asking.

E. M. Bounds, The Weapon of Prayer

A little boy was saying his prayers before bedtime in a very low voice.
"I can't hear you, dear," his mother whispered.
"Wasn't talking to you," said the small one firmly.

Anonymous

We can be addicted to our self-images. For example, I am seduced
and enticed by a certain image of myself as a whole, holy, loving man
who is well on his way to becoming free from attachments. When this
image comes up in my prayer, it causes me to pause and posture; I
find myself trying to make my prayer fit my image of how a holy
man would pray. I no longer really invite God into my prayer. It
becomes an act, a scene I play out for my own edification.

Gerald May, Addiction and Grace

While two pastors' wives sat mending their husbands' pants, one of
them said to the other: "My poor Richard is so discouraged. Nothing seems to go right for him at the church, and he's at the point of
resigning."

The other replied: "My husband is feeling just the opposite. He's more
enthused than ever and senses the Lord's presence in a special way."

A hushed silence fell as they continued to mend the trousers, one patching the seat and the other the knees.

Adapted from James S. Hewett, Illustrations Unlimited

Practical prayer is harder on the soles of your shoes than on the knees of your trousers.

Austin O'Malley

If we do get specific, we zero in on health, transportation, shelter, employment, and other practical concerns of daily life. Not that God is indifferent toward your need for a better car or the missionary's need for an airplane, but the New Testament prayers had a different emphasis.

Wentworth Pike, Principles of Effective Prayer

Our prayers for others flow more easily than those we offer on our own behalf. . . . One [reason] is that I am often, I believe, praying for others when I should be doing things for them. It's so much easier to pray for a bore than to go and see him.

C. S. Lewis, Letters to Malcolm

Preacher: Do you say your prayers at night, Jimmy?
Jimmy: Yes, sir.
Preacher: And do you always say them in the morning, too?
Jimmy: No, sir. I ain't scared in the daytime.

Anonymous

Spontaneity as opposed to formality in prayer has been stressed so much in evangelical circles that we have gone to the other extreme. Our prayers have degenerated into materialistic requests with very little spiritual content or concern for the glory of God. We have given so little attention to the words of our prayers that they are ineffective because they are non-specific: "Lord, bless the pastor and the Sunday School teachers, and bless the missionaries."

Anonymous

There's something exquisitely luxurious about room service in a hotel. All you have to do is pick up a phone and somebody is ready and waiting to bring you breakfast, lunch, dinner, a chocolate milkshake, whatever your heart desires and your stomach will tolerate. Or by another languid motion of the wrist, you can telephone for someone who will get a soiled shirt quickly transformed into a clean one or a rumpled suit into a pressed one. That's the concept that some of us have of prayer. We have created God in the image of a divine bellhop. Prayer, for us, is the ultimate in room service, wrought by direct dialing. Furthermore, no tipping, and everything charged to that great credit card in the sky. Now prayer is many things, but I'm pretty sure this is not one of the things it is.

Kenneth L. Wilson

God hears no more than the heart speaks; and if the heart be dumb, God will certainly be deaf.

Thomas Brooks

Certain thoughts are prayers. There are moments when, whatever be the attitude of the body, the soul is on its knees.

Victor Hugo

God puts our prayers like rose leaves between the leaves of His book of remembrance, and when the volume is opened at last, there shall be a precious fragrance springing from them.

R. G. Lee, Pickings

The fewer the words, the better the prayer.

Martin Luther

The prayer of the righteous is powerful and effective.

James 5:17, NRSV

Talk to him in prayer of all your wants, your troubles, even of the weariness you feel in serving him. You cannot speak too freely, too trustfully, to him.

Francois de la Mothe Fénelon

Seeking Quietness and Solitude

Be still, and know that I am God!

Psalm 46:10, NRSV

Under all speech that is good for anything there lies a silence that is better. Silence is deep as Eternity; speech is shallow as Time.

Thomas Carlyle

True Christian experience must always include a genuine encounter with God. Without this, religion is but a shadow, a reflection of reality, a cheap copy of the original. . . . The spiritual giants of old were men who at some time became acutely conscious of the real Presence of God and maintained that consciousness for the rest of their lives.

A. W. Tozer

Everyone is naturally contemplative. The people we call contemplatives are not unique in their nature; they just have a little extra longing to recover the nature that is common to us all. Scripture tells us that we must become like little children, and that the teaching we need is right here if we have eyes to see and ears to hear. It tells us that we live and move and have our being in a divine One who is already at home in us, ready to guide us where we need to go. It tells us that Holy Wisdom cries in the streets for us, promising that in self-abandonment we will never be abandoned. It assures us that we will find what we seek, that we shall know the truth, and that it will make us free.

Gerald May, in The Shalem Newsletter

Solitude, though it may be silent as light, is like light, the mightiest of agencies; for solitude is essential to man. All men come into this world alone and leave it alone.

Thomas De Quincey

Great priests, saints like the Cure d'Ars, who have seen into the hidden depths of thousands of souls, have, nevertheless, remained men with few intimate friends. No one is more lonely than a priest who has a vast ministry. He is isolated in a terrible desert by the secrets of his fellow men.

Thomas Merton, No Man Is an Island

The Christian way of life does not take away our loneliness; it protects and cherishes it as a precious gift. Sometimes it seems as if we do everything possible to avoid the painful confrontation with our basic human loneliness, and allow ourselves to be trapped by false gods promising immediate satisfaction and quick relief. . . . Our loneliness reveals to us an inner emptiness that can be destructive when misunderstood, but filled with promise for him who can tolerate its sweet pain.

Henri Nouwen, The Wounded Healer

Loneliness expresses the pain of being alone and solitude expresses the glory of being alone.

Paul Tillich

I am only a poor man, accustomed to small things and silence.

Pope John Paul I, Illustrissimi

What a thing it is to sit absolutely alone in the forest at night, cherished by this wonderful, unintelligent perfectly innocent speech, the most comforting speech in the world. . . . Nobody started it, nobody is going to stop it. It will talk as long as it wants, the rain. As long as it talks I am going to listen.

Thomas Merton

If we have not quiet in our minds, outward comfort will do no more for us than a golden slipper on a gouty foot.

John Bunyan

To have a quiet mind is to possess one's mind wholly; to have a calm spirit is to possess one's self.

Hamilton Mabie

Quiet minds cannot be perplexed or frightened but go on in fortune or misfortune at their own private pace, like a clock during a thunderstorm.

Robert Louis Stevenson

It is easy in the world to live after the world's opinions; it is easy in solitude to live after your own; but the great man is he who in the midst of the crowd keeps with perfect sweetness the independence of solitude.

Ralph Waldo Emerson

They always talk who never think, and who have the least to say.

Matthew Prior

An inability to stay quiet is one of the conspicuous failings of mankind.

Walter Bagehot

PASTORAL LIFE

Affirming the Call

At times we try to tame the call by equating a staff position in a church or religious organization with the call itself. But the call always transcends the things we do to earn money, even if those thing are done in the church. . . . If tomorrow I am fired and forced to find employment in the gas station down the street, my vocation would remain intact. I still would be called to preach . . . . No office or position can be equated with the call. No credential, degree, or test should be confused with it. No professional jargon or psycho babble can tame it. No training or experience or ecclesiastical success can replace it. Only the call suffices. Everything else is footnote and commentary.

Ben Patterson, in Leadership Handbooks of Practical Theology

The chief end and duty of man is to love God and to enjoy him forever.

The Westminster Catechism

Vocation: It comes from the Latin *vocare*, to call, and means the work a person is called to by God. There are all different kinds of voices calling you to all different kinds of work, and the problem is to find out which is the voice of God rather than of Society, say, or the Superego, or Self-Interest. . . . The place God calls you to is the place where your deep gladness and the world's deep hunger meet.

Frederick Buechner, Wishful Thinking

That the eyes of all workers should behold the integrity of the work is the sole means to make that work good in itself and so good for mankind. This is only another way of saying that the work must be measured by the standard of eternity; or that it must be done for God first and foremost; or that the Energy must faithfully manifest forth the Idea; or, theologically, that the Son does the will of the Father.

Dorothy Sayers, The Mind of the Maker

Identify your highest skill and devote your time to performing it. Delegate all other skills.

Ronald Brown

To the careerist, work becomes a uniquely intoxicating spirit with which to fill up the glasses and liven up his party/life. His career may contribute significantly to others. But whether it keeps him coming back for more depends on the contribution it makes to himself. The paycheck worth working for is not simply money, but meaning—personal meaning and significance.

Doug Sherman and William Hendricks, Your Work Matters to God

I believe that God made me for a purpose. . . . But he also made me fast. And when I run, I feel his pleasure.

Ian Charleson, in the movie Chariots of Fire

When God wanted sponges and oysters, He made them, and put one on a rock and the other in the mud. When he made man, He did not make him to be a sponge, or an oyster; He made him with feet and hands, head and heart, and vital blood, and a place to use them, and said to him, "Go, work!"

Henry Ward Beecher, Royal Truths

A student at work on his true vocation becomes creative and passionate. A professional whose work comes out of his very soul should almost have to pay instead of being paid for doing that which fills his life with light. Doing things out of obligation, no matter how much effort you put into it, will always be like dragging a ball and chain. Because of this, every man should struggle to love what he does when he cannot do what he loves.

J. L. Martin Descalzo, in Reader's Digest

Maintaining Energy and Zeal

The way to be nothing is to do nothing.

Nathaniel Howe

In my young days, sickly as I was, I could spend ten or even twelve hours at my desk, working all the time; and more than once I worked from four in the morning till four in the afternoon with no more than a cup of coffee . . . and working without pausing for breath. But now I can't do it. In those days I was in control of my own physique and of time itself . . . but now, alas, I can't do it.

Giuseppe Verdi, in a letter to Giulio Ricordi, January 1891

His strength now diminished so much that he found it difficult to preach more than twice a day.

Robert Southey, speaking of the eighty-six-year-old John Wesley

Even if you're on the right track, you'll get run over if you just sit there.

Will Rogers

Sloth, like rust, consumes faster than labor wears, while the used key is always bright.

Benjamin Franklin

Hope for the moment. There are times when it is hard to believe in the future, when we are temporarily just not brave enough. When this happens, concentrate on the present. Cultivate *le petit bonheur* (the little happiness) until courage returns. Look forward to the beauty of the next moment, the next hour, the promise of a good meal, sleep, a book, a movie, the likelihood that tonight the stars will shine and tomorrow the sun will shine. Sink roots into the present until the strength grows to think about tomorrow.

Ardis Whitman, in Reader's Digest

If you do something repeatedly, you lose a little bit of hunger each time. It's up to you to push yourself to regain that hunger.

Michael Jordan

Idleness is an inlet to disorder and makes way for licentiousness. People who have nothing to do are quickly tired of their own company.

Jeremy Collier

That man is idle who can do something better.

Ralph Waldo Emerson

Therefore, since we are surrounded by such a great cloud of witnesses, let us throw off everything that hinders and the sin that so easily entangles, and let us run with perseverance the race marked out for us. Let us fix our eyes on Jesus, the author and perfecter of our faith, who for the joy set before him endured the cross, scorning its shame, and sat down at the right hand of the throne of God. Consider him who endured such opposition from sinful men, so that you will not grow weary and lose heart. In your struggle against sin, you have not yet resisted to the point of shedding your blood.

Hebrews 12:1-4

F. B. Meyer passed the home of C. T. Studd (who was to become a missionary on three continents). He saw a light on in the house incredibly early, so he stopped in. When asked what he was doing up so early, C. T. Studd replied: "Jesus said 'If you love Me, keep My commandments.' So I'm searching the Bible to see if there are any I'm not keeping."

Jim Townsend, Epistles of John and Jude

Never let your zeal outrun your charity. The former is but human, the latter is divine.

Hosea Ballou

Let us not become weary in doing good, for at the proper time we will reap a harvest if we do not give up.

Galatians 6:9

Leading with Openness

Somehow we have come to believe that good leadership requires a safe distance from those we are called to lead. Medicine, psychiatry, and social work all offer us models in which "service" takes place in a one-way direction. Someone serves, someone else is being served, and be sure not to mix up the roles! But how can anyone lay down his life for those with whom he is not even allowed to enter into a deep personal relationship? Laying down your life means making your own faith and doubt, hope and despair, joy and sadness, courage and fear available to others as ways of getting in touch with the Lord of life.

Henri Nouwen, In the Name of Jesus

What you probably feel is the melancholy of happiness. That mood that comes over all of us when we realize that even love can't remain at flood tide forever.

Lionel Barrymore, in the movie Camille

How often we hide behind masks and huge delusions with compulsive passion because we are afraid to be known, to be loved—but in the nearness of real, deep, substantial love we run back to our masks of isolation, shallowness, and safety in terror of being revealed and accepted. We hide ourselves in acts of passion; we buy love under false prudence; we substitute biological pleasures for the divine wonder and peril of love; we surround ourselves with cold, icy barriers to defend the smug self from being shattered by love.

William McNamara, The Art of Being Human

The life of the mind. There's no road map for that territory. Exploring it can be painful. I have a pain most people don't know anything about.

John Turturro, in the movie Barton Fink

I am sure my readers understand the subtle temptation which assails me: that of trying to be the personage I am expected to be. It slips in disguised as an honest concern for the proper fulfillment of my vocation. . . . In order not to disappoint them I ought to tell them only of my positive experiences. In fact they are always disconcerted at first when I speak of my own difficulties, doubts and failings. But they soon come to see that this atmosphere of truth brings us closer and binds us together. My experience of the power of God means more to them than it would if they thought me a quite different sort of person from themselves.

Paul Tournier, The Meaning of Persons

The human heart, at whatever age, opens only to the heart that opens in return.

Marie Edgeworth

There is a tendency in each one of us to deny loneliness. We want to live life independently, no leaning on other people. But a nagging sense of loneliness keeps getting in the way. Sometimes it becomes so severe we can hardly think about anything else. I believe God created us incomplete, not as a cruel trick to edge us toward self-pity, but as an opportunity to edge us toward others with similar needs. His whole plan for us involves relationships with others: reach out to the world around us in love. Loneliness, that painful twinge inside, *makes* us reach out.

Phillip Yancey, Unhappy Secrets of the Christian Life

In order to be a leader a man must have followers. And to have followers, a man must have their confidence. Hence, the supreme quality for a leader is unquestionably integrity. Without it, no real success is possible, no matter whether it is on a section gang, a football field, in an army, or in an office. If a man's associates find him guilty of phoniness, if they find that he lacks forthright integrity, he will fail. His teachings and actions must square with each other. The first great need, therefore, is integrity and high purpose.

Dwight Eisenhower

To be a witness does not consist in engaging in propaganda, nor even in stirring people up; but in being a *living mystery*. It means to live in such a way that one's life would not make sense if God did not exist.

Suhard

The true mentor . . . fosters the young adult's development by believing in him, sharing the youthful dream and giving it his blessing, helping to define the newly emerging self in its newly discovered world, and creating a space in which the young man can work on a reasonably satisfactory life structure. . . . The mentor represents a mixture of parent and peer; he must be both and not purely either one.

Daniel Levinson, The Seasons of a Man's Life

Keep on doing the things that you have learned and received and heard and seen in me, and the God of peace will be with you.

Philippians 4:9, NRSV

Handling those High Expectations

The pastor today is the man on the hot seat. He is supposed to be the man who can do everything. He is supposed to be the visionary for the church. He has to be a strong leader with good business and administrative skills. He has to be entertaining and produce a very thought-provoking sermon every week. He's often in charge of the financial aspects of the church. He's usually responsible for counseling church members with complex personal problems that he may not be equipped to handle. He has to visit the sick and families in which someone has died. He has to preach the funerals and perform the weddings. It's an impossible assignment! It's built for burnout, it's built for exhaustion, and it's built for trouble.

James Dobson, in Ministries Today

Pastor Otto had been in the ministry seven years, but he was "washed up" already. He had tried to be helpful and kind to everyone, but they had "drained him dry." When the ladies forgot to clean up the kitchen, he felt sorry for them and did it himself. When the janitor neglected to sweep the floor and set up the chairs, Otto did it for him. When people shared a problem with him, he carried it as though it were his own. When his denominational treasurer needed more money, he even donated some of his family's food money set aside for the next month! . . . He thought he was being helpful, but, *if you trim yourself to please everyone, you'll soon whittle yourself away*. Don't worry about letting others carry their own responsibility. They will be better people for facing their own failures and deciding what they will do about them. Sometimes it's more helpful not to do the helpful thing.

David Belasic and Paul Schmidt, The Penguin Principles

The trouble with most of us is that we'd rather be ruined by praise than loved by criticism.

Norman Vincent Peale

The classic critic sized up an owl perched in a taxidermist's window for his friends standing with him. The critic blasted the taxidermist: "If I couldn't stuff an owl better than that, I'd quit. The head is awkward, the body-poise isn't right, the feathers are terrible." His friends were rather impressed by the critic's assessment until the owl in the window turned his head and winked.

Jim Townsend, Romans

It is not the critic who counts; not the man who points out how the strong man stumbles, or where the doer of deeds could have done them better. The credit belongs to the man who is actually in the arena, whose face is marred by dust and sweat and blood; who strives valiantly; who errs, and comes short again and again, because there is not effort without error and shortcoming; but who does actually strive to do the deeds; who knows the great enthusiasms, the great devotions; who spends himself in a worthy cause; who at best knows in the end the triumphs of high achievement and who at the worst, if he fails, at least fails while daring greatly, so that his place shall never be with those cold and timid souls who know neither victory nor defeat.

Theodore Roosevelt

Once seminary days are left behind, the woman minister faces many challenges as she begins her professional career. . . . Even after appointment to a pastorate, a woman minister must be prepared to face some problems which are directly related to the fact that she is a woman filling what has been for many centuries a male role. If change is slow in coming about in the seminary, it is even slower at the congregational level.

E. Margaret Howe, Women and Church Leadership

Pastor Gordon was once asked how many active members there were in his church. "One hundred," he replied. "Fifty for me and fifty against me." Gordon had learned the truth of the saying, "Friends may come and go, but enemies accumulate." It's the nature of people. Few of them serve God or others from "pure" motives. No one can even really expect to please more than fifty percent of any group of people for any length of time.

David Belasic and Paul Schmidt, The Penguin Principles

To put it bluntly: No conflict, no story. If we do find a totally satisfactory adjustment in life, we tend to sink into the drowse of the accustomed. Only when our surroundings—or we ourselves—become problematic again do we wake up and feel the surge of energy which is life. And life more abundantly lived is what we seek.

Robert Penn Warren (on writing novels)

Successful leaders dare to be unpopular when they have to make tough decisions . . . and they accept that there may be long periods . . . before the rewards of their efforts finally appear.

Andrew Sherwood

Show me a thoroughly satisfied man and I will show you a failure.

Thomas A. Edison

I would rather lose in a cause that I know some day will triumph than to triumph in a cause that I know some day will fail.

Wendell L. Willkie

The only time you don't fail is the last time you try anything—and it works.

William Strong

Success is simply a matter of luck. Ask any failure.

Earl Wilson

He's no failure. He's not dead yet.

William Lloyd George

The things you learn in maturity aren't simple things such as acquiring information and skills. You learn not to engage in self-destructive behavior. You learn not to burn up energy in anxiety. You discover how to manage your tensions. You learn that self-pity and resentment are among the most toxic drugs. You find that the world loves talent but pays off on character. You come to understand that most people are neither for you nor against you; they are thinking about themselves. You learn that no matter how hard you try to please, some people in this world are not going to love you—a lesson that is at first troubling and then really quite relaxing.

John W. Garner, in Reader's Digest

If at first you don't succeed, you may be at your level of incompetence already.

Laurence J. Peter

If at first you do succeed—try to hide your astonishment.

Harry F. Banks

Preaching: The Lighter Side

"Isn't Rev. So-and-so a deep preacher?" asked a friend.

"Well," replied the other, smiling. "I'll tell you a story. When I was a boy I was amusing myself with some other boys in a pond. Some of them were going farther out than I was disposed to go, and I was frightened. To a man who was passing by I called out, 'Is this pond deep?'

"'No, son,' he replied, 'it's only muddy.'"

Spiros Zodhiates, Illustrations of Bible Truths

A visitor to the Capitol was accompanied by his small son. The little boy watched from the gallery when the House came to order.

"Why did the minister pray for all those men, Pop?"

"He didn't. He looked them over and prayed for the country."

Anonymous

A boyish-looking minister, serving his first church, noticed that one of his flock had been absent from services several Sundays in a row, so he decided to see her and ask the reason.

The woman shook her head and looked at him pityingly. "Son," she said, "you're not old enough to have sinned enough to have repented enough to be able to preach about it."

5100 Quotations for Speakers and Writers

A Native American had attended services one Sunday morning. The sermon which contained very little in the way of spiritual food had been rather loud in spots. The Indian, a good Christian, was not impressed. When asked how he liked the sermon, he said, "High wind, big thunder, no rain."

Spiros Zodhiates, Illustrations of Bible Truths

A dear woman was weeping copiously as she parted with her pastor. "Now, now," said the pastor, "don't cry; the bishop is sending you a good pastor, a much better one."

"But," she wailed, "that's what they told me the last time."

Robert C. Griffith

A minister was talking to a poor woman who worked hard as a cleaning lady. He told her how glad he was to see her in her place in church every Sunday, so attentive to his sermons.

"Yes," she replied, "it is such a rest after a hard week's work to come to church, sit down on the soft cushions, and not think about anything."

Anonymous

Dad criticized the sermon. Mother thought the organist made a lot of mistakes. Sister didn't like the choir's singing. But they all shut up when Billy chipped in, "I think it was a good show for a nickel."

Anonymous

Whenever I say bad things about people outside our church, or good things about people inside our church, those shaking my hand at the door tell me what a fine sermon I have just given them.

George Hall

A well-known preacher delivered a sermon before a congregation in which his wife was a worshiper. When the service was over, he went over to her and asked, "How did I do?"

She replied, "You did fine, only you missed several opportunities to sit down."

Asbury Lenox

The pastor will not be with us for the evening service tonight, and we will have a time of praising the Lord.

Notice in a church bulletin

PERSONAL LIFE

Deepening Self-Awareness

Everyone thinks of changing the world, but no one thinks of changing himself.

Leo Tolstoy

We know what we are, but know not what we may be.

William Shakespeare

This is the very perfection of a man, to find out his own imperfections.

Augustine

A man would not hesitate to spend everything he had—if he only knew the secret of his own heart. If a man could grasp the bliss of his secret he would shed a tear with every breath he breathed.

Shaykh Muhammad Ibn al-Habib

I see now that my feelings of self-importance in the world were misguided. The world can manage perfectly well without me. Realizing that, I have paradoxically found a different sort of importance within myself. The statement of my life has changed from "I am important" to "I am."

Morton Kelsey

Trust not yourself, but your defects to know,
Make use of every friend and every foe.

Alexander Pope

Until you have given up yourself to Him you will not have a real self. . . . The principle runs through all life from top to bottom. Give up yourself, and you will find your real self. Lose your life and you will save it. Submit to death, death of your ambitions and favorite wishes every day and death of your whole body in the end: submit with every fiber of your being, and you will find eternal life. Keep back nothing. Nothing that you have not given away will ever be really yours. Nothing in you that has not died will ever be raised from the dead.

C. S. Lewis, Mere Christianity

All the significant battles are waged within the self.

Sheldon Kopp

To live our life from the point of view of our death is not necessarily a capitulation to despair, to withdrawal, to passivity. Rather, it can become the basis for our being and doing in the world. The more we refuse to look at our own death, the more we repress and deny new possibilities for living. We are all going to die, and our life is a movement to that sure end. Believers find that meditation on this simple fact has a wonderful way of clearing the mind! It enables them to live every single moment with new appreciation and delight. When I say to myself, "This moment may be my last," I am able to see the world with new eyes.

Alan Jones, Soul Making

Preserving Character and Reputation

The best of all the preachers are the men who live their creeds.

Edgar A. Guest

Many a man's reputation would not know his character if they met on the street.

Elbert Hubbard

Let us not say, Every man is the architect of his own fortune; but let us say, Every man is the architect of his own character.

George Dana Boardman

Character is not made in a crisis—it is only exhibited.

Robert Freeman

If I take care of my character, my reputation will take care of itself.

Dwight L. Moody

What we do on some great occasion will probably depend on what we already are; and what we are will be the result of previous years of self-discipline.

H. P. Liddon

The Queen Mary was the largest ship to cross the oceans when it was launched in 1936. Through four decades and a world war she served until she was retired, anchored as a floating hotel and museum in Long Beach, California. During the conversion, her three massive smokestacks were taken off to be scraped down and repainted. But on the dock they crumbled. Nothing was left of the ¾-inch steel plate from which the stacks had been formed. All that remained were more that thirty coats of paint that had been applied over the years. The steel had rusted away. When Jesus called the Pharisees "whitewashed tombs," he meant they had no substance, only an exterior appearance.

Illustrations for Teaching and Preaching

When a man takes an oath, he's holding his own self in his own hands like water. And if he opens his fingers, then he needn't hope to find himself again.

Paul Scofield, in the movie A Man for All Seasons

A reputation once broken may possibly be repaired, but the world will always keep their eyes on the spot where the crack was.

Joseph Hall

No man, for any considerable period, can wear one face to himself, and another to the multitude, without finally getting bewildered as to which may be the true.

Nathaniel Hawthorne

"Who are you?" said the Caterpillar.

This was not an encouraging opening for a conversation. Alice replied, rather shyly, "I—I hardly know, Sir, just at present—at least I know who I was when I got up this morning but I think I must have been changed several times since then."

"What do you mean by that?" said the Caterpillar, sternly. "Explain yourself!"

"I can't explain myself, I'm afraid, Sir," said Alice, "because I'm not myself, you see."

"I don't see," said the Caterpillar.

"I'm afraid I can't put it more clearly," Alice replied very politely, "for I can't understand it myself, to begin with; and being so many different sizes in a day is very confusing."

Lewis Carroll, The Adventures of Alice in Wonderland

Blessed is the man
who does not walk in the counsel of the wicked
or stand in the way of sinners
or sit in the seat of mockers.
But his delight is in the law of the Lord,
and on his law he meditates day and night.
He is like a tree planted by streams of water,
which yields its fruit in season
and whose leaf does not wither.
Whatever he does prospers.

Psalm 1:1-3

A bad man is worse when he pretends to be a saint.

Francis Bacon

If to do were as easy as to know what were good to do, chapels had been churches and poor men's cottages princes' palaces. It is a good divine that follows his own instructions: I can easier teach twenty what were good to be done, than be one of the twenty to follow mine own teaching.

William Shakespeare, Merchant of Venice

The voice that we hear over our shoulders never says, "First be sure that your motives are pure and selfless and then follow me." If it did, then we could none of us follow. So when later the voice says, "Take up your cross and follow me," at least part of what is meant by "cross" is our realization that we are seldom any less than nine parts fake. Yet our feet can insist on answering him anyway, and on we go, step after step, mile after mile. How far? How far?

Frederick Buechner, The Magnificent Defeat

The reputation of a man is like his shadow, gigantic when it precedes him, and pygmy in its proportions when it follows.

Alexandre de Talleyrand-Prigord

Character is what you are in the dark.

Dwight L. Moody

The two most precious things this side of the grave are our reputation and our life. But it is to be lamented that the most contemptible whisper may deprive us of the one, and the weakest weapon of the other.

Charles Caleb Colton

What people say behind your back is your standing in the community.

Ed Howe

Facing Temptation

We are half-hearted creatures, fooling about with drink and sex and ambition when infinite joy is offered us, like an ignorant child who wants to go on making mud pies in a slum because he cannot imagine what is meant by the offer of a holiday at the sea. We are far too easily pleased.

C. S. Lewis, The Weight of Glory

It is precisely the men and women who are dedicated to spiritual leadership who are easily subject to very raw carnality. The reason for this is that they do not know how to live the truth of the Incarnation. They separate themselves from their own concrete community, try to deal with their needs by ignoring them or satisfying them in distant or anonymous places, and then experience an increasing split between their own most private inner world and the good news they announce. When spirituality becomes spiritualization, life in the body becomes carnality.

Henri Nouwen, In the Name of Jesus

Our happiness revolves again and again round the issue of satisfying our desires. We are unhappy when our desires are not met and when, in consequence, we try to make do with less and less. We long . . . for a place where the ego can relax into self-sufficiency.

Alan W. Jones, Soul Making

Most people, if they had really learned to look into their own hearts, would know that they do want, and want acutely, something that cannot be had in this world. There are all sorts of things in the world that offer to give it to you, but they never quite keep their promise.

C. S. Lewis, Mere Christianity

I've looked on a lot of women with lust. I've committed adultery in my heart many times. This is something that God recognizes I will do—and I have done it—and God forgives me for it.

Jimmy Carter

It is as impossible to play with sin and not get burnt . . . as it is to stop bullets on their way to their target with a tennis racket.

R. G. Lee

If you're a typical man, you've tried to deal with your sexual concerns by yourself. You may have friends, but you really don't offer your life to them as an open book with no secrets. We men can be very good at faking our openness by carefully selecting topics that seem candid, yet safe enough. The greatest hater of a man's soul, Satan, knows that his turf is threatened by the safety and power of brotherhood. The forces of evil will do everything they can to separate a man from others, to force him into a place where he's starved for the encouragement, the correction, the prayer—the love—of the men of God.

Brian Peterson, in New Man

The truth about the Christian life seems to be, however, that no one bats a thousand in facing temptation. As a matter of fact, most of the saints felt that their averages were pretty low. We can improve our performance, and I thank God that this is so. But evidently in this life we will always have occasional experience of succumbing to temptation. The sad truth is that much of the time I am too weak to resist, and my failure is simply a hard cold fact with which I must live. I have to come to God with the horribly uncomfortable feeling of failure. And finally, with no excuses, I force myself to my knees before Him in confession, asking for restoration to a state of usefulness and self-acceptance by His grace.

Keith Miller, Habitation of Dragons

Recognizing the Need for Rest

We have clearly lost something when we are no longer free just to be, when we must always be active, doing some things and refraining from doing others. Something is missing when we have to force our pauses, carve out our spaces, and then feel we have to justify them. As a result, recreation often means engaging in more pleasurable work, not freedom from having to work at all.

Gerald May, The Awakened Heart

A life spent in constant labor is a life wasted, save a man be such a fool as to regard a fulsome obituary notice as ample reward.

George Jean Nathan

Rest: the sweet sauce of labor.

Plutarch

There is more to life than increasing its speed.

Mahatma Gandhi

Tripping hither, tripping thither
Nobody knows the why or whither.
If you ask the special function
Of our never ceasing motion,
We reply without compunction
that we haven't any notion.

Anonymous

This is definitely not the hour when men take kindly to an exhortation to listen, for listening is not today a part of popular religion. We are at the opposite end of the pole from there. Religion has accepted the monstrous heresy that noise, size, activity and bluster make a man dear to God. But we may take heart. To a people caught in the tempest of the last great conflict God says, "Be still, and know that I am God," and still He says it, as if He means to tell us that our strength and safety lie not in noise but in silence.

A. W. Tozer, The Pursuit of God

Put off thy cares with thy clothes; so shall thy rest strengthen thy labor, and so thy labor sweeten thy rest.

Francis Quarles

Avoid fried meats which angry up the blood. If your stomach disputes you, lie down and pacify it with cool thoughts. Keep the juices flowing by jangling around gently as you move. Go very light on the vices, such as carrying on in society. The social ramble ain't restful. Avoid running at all times. Don't look back. Something might be gaining on you.

Satchel Paige, How to Stay Young

"What do you do during the day?" a friend asked an elderly Scotch woman who lived alone. "Well," she said, "I get my hymn book and sing. Then I read the Psalms, meditating on God's greatness. When I get tired of reading and cannot sing anymore, I just sit still and let the Lord love me!"

Gary Wilde, Your Ministry of Prayer

The trouble with the rat race is that even if you win, you're still a rat.

Lily Tomlin

Growing in True Humility

Now listen, you who say, "Today or tomorrow we will go to this or that city, spend a year there, carry on business and make money." Why, you do not even know what will happen tomorrow. What is your life? You are a mist that appears for a little while and then vanishes. Instead, you ought to say, "If it is the Lord's will, we will live and do this or that." As it is, you boast and brag. All such boasting is evil.

James 4:13-16

Let us believe neither half of the good people tell us of ourselves, nor half the evil they say of others.

John Petit-Senn

You know, you are very large on religion and all the rest of it, but you don't even know how to accept a gift from somebody without making them feel small.

Sidney Poitier to a nun, in the movie Lilies of the Field

Whatever is done without ostentation, and without the people being witnesses of it, is, in my opinion, most praiseworthy: not that the public eye should be entirely avoided, for good actions desire to be placed in the light; but notwithstanding this, the greatest theater for virtue is conscience.

Cicero

To Mr. John Trembath, Tiverton, September 21, 1775:

I observed long ago that you are not patient of reproof; and I fear you are less so now than ever. But since you desire it, I will tell you once more what I think concerning you. I think you tasted of the powers of the world to come thirteen or fourteen years ago and were then simple of heart and willing to spend and be spent for Christ. But not long after, not being sufficiently on your guard, you suffered loss by being applauded. This revived and increased your natural vanity, which was the harder to be checked because of your innate stubbornness. . . . First, recover the life of God in your own soul and walk as Christ walked. Walk with God as you did twelve years ago. Then you might again be useful to His children.

John Wesley, reproving a young minister in a letter

Two ministers of different denominations were the best of friends, but often disagreed on religious issues. One day they had been arguing a little more than usual on some theological point, when one of them said: "That's all right. We'll just agree to disagree. The thing that counts is that we're both doing the Lord's work—you in your way, and I in His."

Clyde Murdock

Get someone else to blow your horn and the sound will carry twice as far.

Will Rogers

It is unwise to be too sure of one's own wisdom. It is healthy to be reminded that the strongest might weaken and the wisest might err.

Mahatma Gandhi

I have great faith in fools—self-confidence my friends call it.

Edgar Allan Poe

Even on the most exalted throne in the world we are only sitting on our own bottom.

Michel de Montaigne